A Big Youth Ministry Topic

THE SKINNY

ON

SERVICE

Tony Myles

with Doug Franklin

Group

The Skinny on Service
© 2015 Tony Myles

group.com
simplyyouthministry.com

Credits
Authors: Tony Myles with Doug Franklin
Executive Developer: Tim Gilmour
Executive Editor: Rick Lawrence
Chief Creative Officer: Joani Schultz
Editor: Rob Cunningham
Art Director and Cover Art: Veronica Preston
Cover Photography: Rodney Stewart
Production: Joyce Douglas
Project Manager: Stephanie Krajec

ISBN 978-1-4707-2090-2
10 9 8 7 6 5 4 3 2 1   21 20 19 18 17 16 15

Printed in the United States of America.

ACKNOWLEDGMENTS

Somebody serves me beyond what I deserve every day.

This is the section where I as a writer should formally thank them. The reality is that I should actually thank them in person. Assuming I've covered that, I'll let this be the icing on the cake.

My wife, Katie, for example, makes a hot breakfast sandwich for me to eat each week as I head out the door to serve our church. That's after I've put on clothes she's washed, dried, folded, and hung up... after showering in a bathroom she's cleaned in spots I'll never, ever fully notice (even if I really try)...after sleeping in a bed she's made for us to sleep in, and so on. Maybe that's not fantastic enough to mention in a book on serving, or maybe it's perfect. I'm only skimming the surface of how she's a Proverbs 31 woman and is helping me raise phenomenal kids—Joshua, Daniel, and Johanna—whose faith and willingness to serve overshadows our own.

I wasn't raised a Christian, though. That means I always need to remember I am where I am today because of a volunteer-intensive student ministry I walked into as a teenager who helped me to become a Christ-follower. Taking into account friends, mentors, and more over the years, I owe more than I could ever repay to Roddy

Chiong, Rob Murphy, Dan Webster, Tony Schwartz, Bo Boshers, Bud Bence, Larry Mitchell, Mark Oestreicher, Rick Lawrence, Kami Gilmour, and more—including my good friends at Group Publishing, Simply Youth Ministry, and Group Missions.

Last but not least, thanks to any church that gave me a shot to make a fool of myself serving Jesus. Every pat on the back or paycheck with my name on it meant you had faith in me to help you have faith in God. Even when you drove me inappropriately crazy, you helped me better define what it meant to be appropriately insane for the Lord. May I continue to be one you regard as a servant of Christ, and as one entrusted with the mysterious, plain truths of God.

—Tony Myles

CONTENTS

THE SKINNY

ON

SERVICE

BEFORE YOU GET STARTED

The book you're holding might be "skinny," but that's because it's all-muscle. This means that Tony Myles and Doug Franklin have cut away the fat and focused on the "first things" that make service in youth ministry powerful and long-lasting. In our Skinny Books series, we've paired a thought leader (in this case, Tony Myles) with a master practitioner (in this case, Doug Franklin) as a one-two punch. We want you to be challenged and equipped in both your thinking and your doing.

And, as a bonus, we've added an Introduction written by Dave Livermore that explores service through the filter of a Jesus-centered approach to ministry. Jesus-centered is much more than a catchphrase to us—it's a passionate and transformative approach to life and ministry. Dave's Introduction to service first appeared in my book *Jesus-Centered Youth Ministry,* and we couldn't think of a better way to kick off this little book. It's time to get skinny...

—RICK LAWRENCE
Executive Editor of Group Magazine

THE SKINNY

ON

SERVICE

INTRODUCTION

Here's something that sounds obvious: Jesus must be central to how we engage youth in service. But what does that really mean? How is the service done by a Jesus-centered youth ministry different from service done by any group of teenagers? Something ought to clearly set apart our service as Christ-followers. At the heartbeat of Jesus-centered service is a proactive commitment to look at how Jesus himself served and engaged in mission.

To understand how Jesus served, we have to look at the backstory in the Old Testament. Particularly from Exodus onward, it's very clear that God's ears are tuned first and foremost to the cry of the oppressed. We see this most clearly when God rescues his people from the heavy hand of the Egyptian empire (Exodus 3 and following). In turn, God calls his people to do the same on his behalf with other nations by becoming a "kingdom of priests" (Exodus 19).

Though Israel does a less than stellar job in its "priestly" role, it's through Israel that Jesus comes on the scene. God himself shows up in the flesh to rescue all of humanity. And through Jesus, we get to see how God looks, thinks, acts, and serves. Essentially, we get to see God the Rescuer with skin on. Jesus becomes the living expression of the mission God had originally given to Israel.

And as Jesus is resurrected to the Father's right hand, the disciples are left to continue his mission of rescuing. Even though Jesus' earthly ministry is "over," God continues to wear his skin through the body of Christ—the church. God designed us to be his agents of redemption who rescue people personally and from systems of injustice. So what does it look like for our youth ministries to give people living experiences with the rescuing God? More and more youth ministries are incorporating acts of kindness and compassion as central to their service and missions projects. Some groups debate about whether these expressions are true expressions of the gospel. Most of our brothers and sisters in the non-Western church are perplexed that we even waste time arguing about this—the gospel *must* be proclaimed and embodied.

The more we spend time looking at Jesus, both personally and with our youth, the more compelled we will be to get up and extend the rescuing arm of God to the plight of those around us, near and far. Look around you. God has skin!

> —Dave Livermore
> *President of the Cultural Intelligence Center*

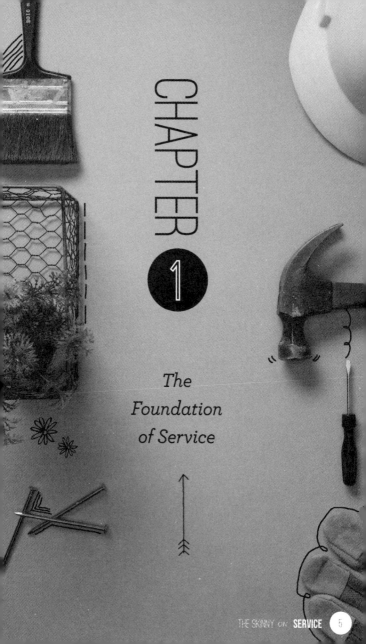

CHAPTER 1

*The
Foundation
of Service*

THE SKINNY

ON

SERVICE

Some readers are probably just skimming the words of these opening pages.

I wouldn't blame you if you did that. When I was new in ministry, I needed ideas FAST. Like you, I would have considered skipping this foundational section to move on to the "nuts and bolts" later in the book.

Still, while I have your attention, can I use a single word to talk you into staying?

Huperetes.

You may not recognize that word, but you've likely read it in the New Testament. It's the original Greek word underneath the word *servants* found in most modern translations of 1 Corinthians 4:1.

> *"This, then, is how you ought to regard us: as servants of Christ and as those entrusted with the mysteries God has revealed" (NIV).*

That's actually rather fitting. I'll explain as we quickly move through this first section.

WHO IS SERVING ULTIMATELY FOR?

The word *huperetes* means "under-oarsman." It refers to the servants on a boat in its hidden galley who pulled huge oars that extended out of the ship into the waters.

The unique thing about an under-oarsman is that from the outside looking in, you never saw these servants. You simply saw the work itself being done and the progress it afforded the ship against the great, sweeping waters. To coordinate these efforts, a drummer would set a tempo for everyone rowing.

As Christ-followers, Jesus sets our pace based on how he lived and taught. His rhythm affirms that impact in the kingdom of God is not attained through status, success, or stability. Rather, it's as much a conscious act of the will for us as it was for Christ to offer a humble, selfless spirit of serving. Like the under-oarsmen, our work—and not us—should be seen.

Blah, blah, blah.

You know this, right?

But when you give up your time, do you acknowledge that it was God's time to begin with? Do you know what it means to operate with such submission and humility that you don't even think about how submissive and humble you're being? Have you yet mastered what it means to step *into* the spotlight to rally others, in order to quickly step *out of* the spotlight so they don't follow you but follow Jesus?

The under-oarsmen never received any glory. While the red carpet was rolled out for the captain or king, the under-oarsmen stayed hidden on the bottom of the boat.

Chew on that, because Jesus can be hidden by Christians who serve for attention or who demand a red carpet ceremony for their good deeds. Instead of hiding him, we're called to hide ourselves and let every act of genuine Christian service point to Christ's ultimate act of service on the cross. It's his compelling presence that attracts people and transforms the world—not just our actions or words.

- How many serving experiences or mission trips have you seen easily become about someone wanting to experience some sort of spiritual "high"?

- What's the difference between someone who serves without seeking recognition and someone who wants to make sure they get some acknowledgement for it?

Serving is about doing something for someone else without other people finding out about it. It's ultimately for Jesus Christ, and practically for the person or cause we're attempting to further.

Nod your head at that. And then consider what it means to nod your life and ministry toward it, too.

Then again, it's really not your ministry anyway. It doesn't even belong to your teenagers or your church, but to God himself:

> "For everything comes from him and exists by his power and is intended for his glory. All glory to him forever! Amen" (Romans 11:36).

WHEN IS THE BEST TIME TO SERVE?

The Bible offers various criteria on when someone should take on a position of spiritual leadership. When it comes to simply serving, however, everyone has the capacity to do something at any given time.

Once when the disciples came to Jesus complaining that someone was doing things they thought only their group should do, Jesus replied, "Don't stop him! Anyone who is not against you is for you" (Luke 9:50).

That means there's no limit regarding who can serve or what a servant looks like.

Anyone can serve—anyone.

Anyone can be served—anyone.

It's why you can take a non-Christian kid on a mission trip and watch his heart enlarge for God as he sits in a pile of trash next to an orphan.

It's why you can take a churched kid on the same trip and watch her realize she's there to lead her non-Christian friend to Jesus instead of you doing it.

It's also why one of Jesus' most frequently asked questions was a variation of, "What can I do for you?"[1] The Savior seemed to have no issue doing something right then and there for the person who needed something done. Imagine if you made that the question you were known for asking on a regular basis. What would happen next? Would it ever get out of hand?

That's where *your* spiritual leadership and discernment matter.

WHERE DOES IT MAKE SENSE TO SERVE FIRST?

Your students certainly can begin serving by responding to needs in front of them. It's likely that adults are currently doing things in your ministry that teenagers could do instead. Teenagers can ultimately be entrusted with coordinating groups, organizing activities, running multimedia, overseeing follow-up efforts, leading games, and so much more.

Of course, there is value to processing things internally before serving externally. This is true for teenagers as much as it is for adults, whether serving visibly in upfront roles or doing the "hidden" jobs nobody else wants to do. Set the tone for this, perhaps by using two other biblical concepts from Greek works to offer your students context...

A WAITER: *Diakonos* refers to "one who serves," much like the role of a waiter in a dining experience. That person's availability, attitude, expressions, and words should ultimately complement the needs of the guests and not distract them. Good waiters do this by using their whole bodies to serve and by employing a solid sense of timing on when to approach or withdraw. The "best of the best" waiters come across as always available yet intentionally unnoticed.

Likewise, true servants in the kingdom of God know how to walk alongside others and quietly take care of whatever is needed. In fact, *diakonos* is the root for the word *deacon*—a concept not about power and authority, but about love dressed in work clothes. When we serve through our actions and words, it's like we're filling up and passing out cups of cool water that refresh others:

- "I prayed for you this morning. How are you really doing?"

- "Let me get the door for you."

- "What's the dirtiest job that needs to be done? Can I do it?"

A CIVIL SERVANT: *Leitourgos* (Romans 15:16) biblically refers to someone who serves the needs of their fellow man (and woman). In ancient Greece, people with resources would volunteer to care for certain state duties called "liturgies"—and they did it at their own expense. It wasn't meant to advance them in status, but to advance the greater good.

We do this when we share the riches we have in Christ with others, or when we come alongside to meet people's physical needs through the resources God has given us. Perhaps that's why the word *liturgy* became our reference for what happens in a worship service. The purest meaning of this word is about generously sowing a seed into a culture or group of people with no strings attached. It's moving from "I scratch your back, you scratch mine" to "I scratch your back."

- "Someone has to get this going and supply the resources for it to happen. No one else is stepping up. I'll be that person, if even just for this first season to inspire others."

- "Those kids won't make it to youth group unless someone regularly picks them up. Let me find a van and a driver."

- "We need several things we currently don't have if we want an effective youth program. Let's all take part in a door-to-door fundraiser."

❯ A VETERAN LEADER'S PERSPECTIVE Doug Franklin

Teenagers can do a lot more than most people allow them to handle. Many times their "limits" are boundaries that adults and culture have placed on them, instead of the potential that a limitless God has placed inside of them. Churches often view youth ministry as the church's ministry to students, but it also must involve our students' ministry to the world. Are they serving Christ, or are they being served? Have they been able to sit in the midst of God's many teachable moments that come from these opportunities, or have they watched from the sidelines? As Christ-followers we are all servants of the king—no matter how old, how experienced, or how mature. Let's make sure we don't hold teenagers back from a critical part of their spiritual formation by restricting their potential to serve.

WHY IS SERVING EVEN IMPORTANT?

You may not want to hear this, but I'll say it anyway.

Serving others creates the opportunity to verbally tell them about Jesus.

There's a different concept tossed around in some circles, though. It's on everything from bumper stickers to T-shirts: *"Preach the gospel at all times. Use words if necessary."*

That's clever, isn't it? Many people like it because it's like an escape clause out of actually having to tell others about their faith. It's often attributed to St. Francis of Assisi, although the closest thing he said to it was this:

> *"No brother should preach contrary to the form and regulations of the holy Church nor unless he has been permitted by his minister ... All the Friars ... should preach by their deeds."*[2]

In other words, we *are* to preach—and when we preach, our lives must back up what our words talk about. Accordingly, the things we do should create opportunities for us to also speak to others about Jesus.

I told you that you might not want to hear this.

- Wouldn't it be a whole lot easier to take your students on an annual trip to just do good deeds somewhere?

- Doesn't it sound more exciting to shoot a highlight video of how you built a house from start-to-finish instead of sitting down with people and making sure they know Jesus as Savior and Lord?

A few years ago, our church pulled off an amazing day of serving a low-income apartment complex. I walked around and felt proud of every station of the miniature carnival we'd brought in, from games and snow cones to free haircuts and backpacks with school supplies. But that's when it hit me: We'd done everything except mention the name of Jesus or explain how he was our motivation for all of it.

Atheists could've done what we did.

Serving is meant to be an on-ramp to the highway. By itself, an on-ramp has no point other than creating a "high" that you must eventually come down from. But when connected to the "high way" of articulating Jesus with your words, serving can forge a journey for everyone that lasts for the long haul.

Take a look around at this world's brokenness and spiritual poverty. God wants to change all of that and is looking for men, women, teenagers, and kids who want that change to start in them.

Serving is how all of that oozes out.

⊘ A VETERAN LEADER'S PERSPECTIVE *Doug Franklin*

In our effort to avoid alienating people with overly "spiritual" words, we may have swung the pendulum too far in the opposite direction. Acts of service fit comfortably into a culture focused on social justice, while God's redemption story may be on the social outs. Most students think it's easier to serve than to tell others about Jesus.

Our teenagers may be growing as effective servants, but are their words just as effective? Can our students articulate their own faith stories within God's overarching redemption narrative? Do they recognize others' need for a Savior? What about their own need for a Savior? Service should flow out of this larger gospel story. Remember, teenagers are capable of more than just inviting friends to church; they can communicate Jesus' message to those friends—maybe even better than we can.

THE SKINNY

ON

SERVICE

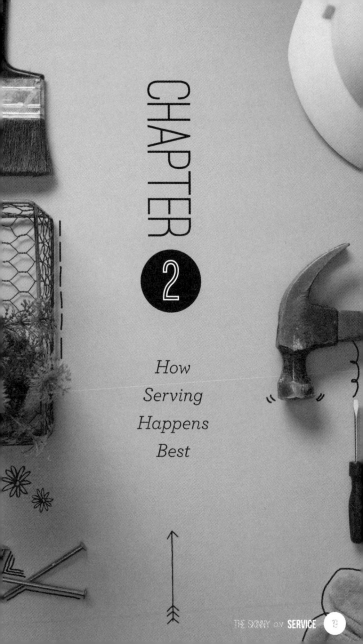

CHAPTER 2

*How
Serving
Happens
Best*

THE SKINNY SERVICE

Every teenager in the van must have been filled with adrenaline.

Larry said he was going to punch Josh in the face.

That was right after Josh called Larry a fat idiot.

Moments before that, Larry had announced to everyone in the van that Josh had "zero taste in music." Josh, as usual, had given Larry that ammunition by asking to hear some "old school" MxPx again.

It was the seventh day of a 10-day mission trip across five states, stopping to serve from place to place. My wife and I, along with 10 students, had taken over a 12-passenger van that barely held together and had no air conditioning.

Let me say that again: teenagers packed into a van for several days in a row without air conditioning—in July.

Every student had an agenda for our music.

Josh whined, "Is it FINALLY time for me to get to pick?"

Larry mumbled something about shutting him up for good. He really seemed like he was going to get violent with Josh. I could feel the tension growing as one of the high school girls went into her own happy space and began repeating, "PLEASE! PLEASE! PLEASE!"

I'd had enough.

We exited the highway and pulled into a gas station parking lot. All I said was, "EVERYBODY! OUT OF THE VAN!"

I didn't have a plan. I only had frustration. So I prayed. It sounds cliché, I know, but I prayed. Somehow in that moment, God broke my heart for what had happened.

I began weeping uncontrollably and had to wait a few minutes before I could even exit the van and face the students.

I asked, "What are we arguing over? How we're going to save lost people? A way to reach a friend who feels like his life is over? What we should do about what's happening in some of your families? NO! WE'RE ARGUING OVER MUSIC! And honestly, I can't think of anything else I can say other than to point that out. When you're ready to get back in the van and remember why we're on this trip, I'll be in there waiting."

Eventually, they did.

An awkward silence took over the evening as we made our way to where we were staying for the night. By morning, three of the girls on the trip who hated conflict made sure everyone apologized to my wife and me. No one talked about music for the rest of the trip.

I told you *that* story to set the stage for this *next* one...

SO, HOW DOES SERVING BEST HAPPEN?

Every one of the disciples must have been filled with adrenaline.

Peter had just been restored by Jesus.

That was right after Thomas had called the other disciples liars.

And then Peter was comparing if he and John would die the same way. John, as usual, had given Peter ammunition by being the teacher's pet.

It all happened during Jesus' 40-day Resurrection Tour. He had somehow brought together the remaining disciples who'd barely held together during the conditions that led to his death. With that context in mind, now read these words:

> "So when the apostles were with Jesus, they kept asking him, 'Lord, has the time come for you to free Israel and restore our kingdom?'

> "He replied, 'The Father alone has the authority to set those dates and times, and they are not for you to know. But you will receive power when the

Holy Spirit comes upon you. And you will be my witnesses, telling people about me everywhere—in Jerusalem, throughout Judea, in Samaria, and to the ends of the earth'" (Acts 1:6-8).

Can you appreciate the raw energy Jesus was dealing with? Here he stood before these young men—he was resurrected and alive after being dead.

Every one of these followers had an agenda for him.

Jesus had had enough.

Thankfully, he had more than frustration. Thankfully, he had a plan.

JESUS-CENTERED RIPPLES

Just before he physically left earth, Jesus explained a four-point strategy to reach the world. His followers could progressively move from one area to the next—ultimately, reaching all people in all places.

It was the best outreach plan ever.

You and I are the evidence. Here we are, processing all of this in some random "ends of the earth" area well outside of where Jesus walked and ministered and spoke all of this. The values of the plan he gave the disciples are values we can follow, as are the ripples we can experience if serving always begins with Jesus somehow.

❯ A VETERAN LEADER'S PERSPECTIVE *Doug Franklin*

Jesus doesn't need us. God is capable of accomplishing his mission without enlisting a ragtag group of bumbling humans. Yet God wanted to give us a peek behind the curtain so we could stand in awe of him. For some reason, we (and our students) serve from the mindset that God really needs our help. Don't get me wrong, obedience is good—but a God who can't do his job without you is no God at all. And that's exciting! God isn't forced to use you—God wants your help.

It's common for teenagers to gain a sense of self-importance when they serve. They begin making reckless decisions that don't rely on wisdom, prayer, or the Holy Spirit. Help students see the Great Commission as an invitation into the adventure of a lifetime that is way above our heads and beyond our ability. This view brings teenagers to their knees in prayer. It makes room for the Holy Spirit to do the unexpected, and it keeps students returning from service trips from feeling jobless in their daily routines.

JESUS: The disciples obeyed Jesus and didn't head out in their own enthusiasm but waited for the Spirit. This mattered for Jesus' plan to have any long-lasting impact.

Maybe it's because he offers a vision of the way things could be for every person of every age. Perhaps he simply wants our

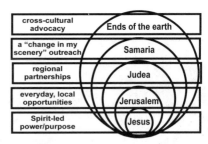

cross-cultural advocacy	Ends of the earth
a "change in my scenery" outreach	Samaria
regional partnerships	Judea
everyday, local opportunities	Jerusalem
Spirit-led power/purpose	Jesus

hearts intertwined with his and one another as we serve.

So Jesus' disciples prayed. It sounds cliché, I know, but they prayed. If you skip this step in your serving process, you just may end up doing something out of obligation or adrenaline. You will only lead from your values and impart those principles to students, like good morals you've sprayed with holy cologne. Instead, God wants to break your heart and let you uncontrollably weep for what he wants to happen. In doing so, you become open to the Holy Spirit leading you and your serving efforts with power and purpose.

- **Why do you think Jesus didn't just physically stick around but instead left so the Spirit could come and dwell within us?**

- **How are you tempted to skip the Spirit and do good deeds that make sense to your own understanding and plans?**

JERUSALEM: There are needs in your own youth group, church, households, and hometown that need to be met. Don't be farsighted and overlook them, opting instead to send teenagers "somewhere else." It's shortsighted to give them the freedom to do things on trips that you won't let them do in-house or in their own backyard.

Jesus wants to rescue the spiritually lost people right in front of you. Teenagers can discover a way to reach a friend who feels his or her life is over. Something can be done regarding the stuff that's happening in some of your students' families. Christ's strategy is to provide the first taste of serving through what's right in front of you. Is that your strategy, too?

- **Where are the deepest pockets of pain in your community?**

- **What is one thing you could do to make young people more aware of the everyday needs they've become used to overlooking?**

JUDEA: Every "Jerusalem" has a "Judea"—the next area over, or the regional territory that impacts your direct community. Think of it like the way a city and a suburb might influence each other. Every region will have trending needs, as well as someone who is attempting to serve those needs.

For example, if you have a high number of teen pregnancies in your area, then it might make sense to partner with a local Christian crisis pregnancy center—or help start one. If there's an alarming rise in bullying, you could connect with school districts and local initiatives that are committed to seeing things change. Identify these needs and begin forming a partnership with others who want to see change happen, too.

- **Who in your region is passionate about solving something that your teenagers are passionate about, too?**

- **How can you create a relationship with other youth ministries and begin to serve alongside them as a larger force for Jesus in your area?**

SAMARIA: At some point you have to get outside of your own comfort zone. Samaria is just that: a new circle that's a change in your scenery, yet still a part of your overall culture. You may not understand it, and at times may even despise it based on your perceptions of it. It's easy to simply conclude that "those people aren't like us."

If you're in the American Midwest, it might mean a trip to the East Coast or West Coast. If you're in area with a noticeable accent, try traveling somewhere where people speak and think much differently than "y'all" do. As Billy Graham explained, "It could be that one of the greatest hindrances to evangelism today is the poverty of our own experience."[3]

- **How could you begin to "listen" to what's happening around the country without stereotyping it or turning people into one-dimensional problems to be fixed?**

- **Where could you take a road trip to help teens experience different cultures within your culture—a place where things still feel familiar on some level but with a different demographic or perspective on another level?**

ENDS OF THE EARTH: There are more needs in our world than you will ever be able to address. But that doesn't mean you can't become a cross-cultural advocate for some issue or cause. You can find at least one foreign part of the world that you can actively care about, pray for, support, and send teams to.

Some people might argue that mission trips or projects don't accomplish anything over the long haul. My word of caution: Don't listen to data on this from people who haven't personally taken more than one cross-cultural trip. Instead, invite them into whatever you're doing so they can give God a chance to break their hearts and personally mold how they see the world.

- **Which area of the world captures the interest of most or many of your teenagers?**

- **What ministries could your students connect with to keep track of and hear regular updates on how their involvement is paying off?**

A process like this gives teenagers a taste of serving and sharing their faith at one level before they progress into the next. An obvious benefit is they can take steps forward as they get more comfortable. A hidden benefit is they don't just go on a trip "somewhere else" without having a foundation of engagement where they live. Students may even begin to notice needs around them, even if it's just one more peer who they otherwise would have overlooked.

Sensitivity, if you will.

Is this the one thing that's missing in your approach to missions? Are the youth around you just chasing down the next high from the next trip? Might some type of strategy like this give you the forethought needed for the future to help kids think about sharing Jesus today?

Do you really believe God wants to pour transformation out...*everywhere*?

Before you answer, consider some of the tensions you'll encounter in making this whole concept work for you like it did for the disciples.

⊙ A VETERAN LEADER'S PERSPECTIVE *Doug Franklin*

Common sense says to teach teenagers about service by starting them on something simple, like setting up chairs for church or helping out in nursery. After all, if they really want to serve, they can do it right here. But that doesn't work with this generation. The last generation may have served out of duty, but today's students serve out of visible impact. For students, impact means caring for people in life-or-death situations: providing clean water for people in the developing world, bringing hope to a child orphaned by AIDS, or freeing sex slaves halfway around the globe. When teenagers tackle these problems, they feel like their service makes a difference.

Yet a life of service should reach from major humanitarian impact all the way down to daily activity. Jesus came to earth for a global rescue mission, but that didn't stop him from serving in the smaller parts of life, like turning water into wine for a wedding celebration. His life was saturated with service.

Our students' lives can be saturated with service, too. We can engage them through service opportunities that yield dramatic impact, but then we must show them that serving in smaller ways can have major impact, too. Push your teenagers to be more than social media activists. Teach them to live as servants, following Jesus' example.

SPONTANEITY VS. STRATEGY

In my experience, the average youth worker struggles with either being too spontaneous or too strategic with serving projects and opportunities. If you're the former, you'll tend to frustrate kids or families who need structure (not to mention your overall church leadership). If you're the latter, you'll end up frustrated when students begin drifting into tangents (which they often do) or when the unexpected happens as you attempt to serve (which it often does).

You must hold both of these values in tension with each other for effective ministry to happen. That's what we see in Acts 1 and 2. Jesus didn't just send the disciples off with a geographical strategy but made sure they first were in an interactive relationship with the Holy

Spirit. Likewise, he didn't give them their supernatural indwelling and then declare, "Now, just go wing it." Both spontaneity and strategy were needed so that when the perfect strategy encountered resistance from an imperfect world, Jesus' followers could still chart a pathway through it, forged and led by God himself.

Take a look at this chart and gauge which side of things you tend to err on most:

I/we tend to come up with big ideas and then improvise along the way.	I/we tend to plan out the details of something before even attempting to do it.
I/we regularly pause to more clearly notice and understand the way things and people really are.	I/we regularly pause to more clearly notice and understand the way things/people can become what/who God desires them to be.
I/we seem available to whatever opportunities end up popping up.	I/we nurture specific serving opportunities in advance through consistent planning.
I/we prefer student-led discovery and randomness that demonstrate ministry ownership.	I/we prefer youth worker-led planning and intentionality that demonstrate sound thinking.
I/we let youth take on ministry as they want. It's OK if they're not in the perfect role. They'll figure it out.	I/we develop systems to make sure students serve in the area they're best in. It's better to not have them waste their time doing something they're not wired for.

I/we would rather walk the streets with students and knock on random doors to find opportunities where we could serve.	I/we would rather join up with an organization that's done its homework to create serving experiences that allow people to know what they're getting into.
I/we tend to have money to spend flexibly on the project while it's happening as we feel it needs to be spent.	I/we operate out of an itemized budget so we can have what we need when we need it and not spend more than what we have.

Remember that one side of the spectrum isn't always better than the other. Both are needed for effective serving to happen. It's why every time in the Bible that Jesus had spontaneous compassion on someone, he immediately followed it with a specific strategy and action plan to meet that person's deepest needs.

If you can process this, you'll begin to recognize the real ministry opportunities God has for you and your team. You might find that the people you intend to impact are secondary to your group members who are yearning to know that God loves them. What if your plans to do great ministry for other people who need to hear about Jesus got in the way of doing great ministry for your own people who need to hear about Jesus?

- **IF STRATEGY IS WHERE YOU STRUGGLE:**
  You likely will have a tough time with advance

communication that helps families and students know about an opportunity and the vision behind it. Many parents won't feel comfortable letting their kids go on trips or take part in student leadership, and your leaders will look to you for answers as questions arise because they have no clue what's going on. When a day of ministry is over, participants will probably be able to tell you *what* they did but not know *why* they did it.

- **IF SPONTANEITY IS WHERE YOU STRUGGLE:** You won't know what to do if someone you didn't plan on serving ends up having an attitude or issues that distract your group. You'll also be more inclined to "lose it" if things don't go as planned or if the pace of serving doesn't ease up. You might even experience confusion over the random opportunities that present themselves on the way to your intended opportunities, such as the time Jesus served a sick woman when he was on his way to heal another person's daughter.[4]

Structure and spontaneity need each other. It's why Jesus talked about the Spirit and strategy in the same moment. Give teenagers and adults the plan in advance, not so they can cling to it but so they can use it to better mine out how God actually intends on working.

Whatever random thoughts God has are better than our best forethought. When an intelligent framework is in place, intelligent freedom can occur.

That leads into another tension worth considering.

DOING THE SAME THING VS. MIXING IT UP

God is always reliable, but he's never predictable.

Do you understand the difference?

Unfortunately, we live in a culture where people might feel the opposite about church and the experiences we offer. They might say we're always predictable, but never reliable.

Ouch.

Perhaps serving can help solve that.

Critics aside, there is a much deeper reason to consider this tension. If teenagers begin to feel that ministry is predictable, they'll unconsciously assume that God is predictable. They may still have one amazing experience after another serving until they graduate from high school, but they will emerge as adults who presume they've tamed God like they tamed ministry.

Maybe you need to deepen their experiences.

Perhaps you should mix things up.

Again, Jesus' plan is Jerusalem AND Judea AND Samaria AND the ends of the earth.

Think about how this *doesn't* play out in youth groups that build their entire year around one particular mission trip. They've mastered the art of fundraising and planning for it, especially because every student knows it's "the thing" they'll do that year. But if you were to pull that trip away, the ministry and its people likely would be confused about what to do next. Perhaps unconsciously, that ministry is making teenagers depend more on the trip than on Jesus.

Certain serving experiences, trips, and outreach efforts will "fit" your group more than other endeavors will. A few may only click for a season, as every year you graduate a group of students out of the ministry and welcome a new group of personalities into it. Negotiating the tension of whether you should do the same thing all the time or ad lib it all each year is revealed in everything from your weekly serving opportunities to your larger investments:

- **SMALL SHIFTS:** Modifying what you're already doing is a safe way to experiment because you may not encounter significantly dramatic consequences. For example, you can vary your serving to a different timeslot or week to mix up who is able to take part and whom you're able to serve. Also consider splitting students into older and younger groups to give each their own space and double the serving opportunities.

  - **What are some small shifts your ministry could make?**

- **MODERATE SHIFTS:** Perhaps you've found one primary serving organization that your group enjoys annually working with, but you might gain value in shifting locations each year. Likewise, identify which of the geographical ripples—Jerusalem, Judea, Samaria, or ends of the earth—is the best description of that project and then add another serving experience that will be different and complementary. If you're looking for a more ongoing moderate shift, challenge your students to volunteer at least once a month in whatever roles are required for your church's weekend services to happen. This can be an entirely student-led Sunday, or it can simply involve them coming alongside the existing leaders in a support role.

- **What are some moderate shifts your ministry could make?**

- **BIG SHIFTS:** Just because you went on an organized mission trip last summer doesn't mean you can't create your own road trip or camp experience this summer. Maybe the very nature of how you gather every week could include some take-home dimension to help teenagers discover how to serve their families. Big shifts involve realizing you don't have to keep doing what you've always done, and this often means asking, "What if instead we..." and then following through.

- **What are some big shifts your ministry could make?**

An easy way to nurture and navigate all of this is to regularly invest in your volunteers and parents. Their unique personalities, perspectives, and passions can overlap and interact and give fresh insight to whatever you've been doing or could be doing. This isn't just about sending them things to read or online surveys to fill out. It's about gathering them together and developing a community where they know their ideas can be freely shared. Structured meetings are fine, as are informal gatherings around a campfire or cookout. Serve people like this, and they'll often serve back by owning their ideas.

The bottom line is that it's OK to frequently re-evaluate your own expectations of what you want serving to feel like. That's a huge part of one other tension.

❯ A VETERAN LEADER'S PERSPECTIVE *Doug Franklin*

Sometimes a great way to mix it up is to pass the leadership to students. God can do amazing things through the eyes of a teenager. Consider putting a small group of students in charge of the next service opportunity. Give them the basic guidelines, and let them go to town. Instead of planning meetings, schedule check-in meetings where they report their plans to you. Let students get their hands dirty and experience the real cost and benefits of leading in God's kingdom. Teenagers who have led real service opportunities in junior high and high school think differently about their kingdom potential in the future. If you can't put students in charge of an entire service opportunity, consider putting them in charge of something smaller, like the messaging or vision casting. Have them create a commercial, ad designs, web graphics, or whatever else they can dream of to get the word out.

BEFORE VS. AFTER

It feels good to look at something and see how it's
now different because you spent a day working on it.
But simply filling holes and digging new ones without
knowing why—that just doesn't hold much appeal. We
like to know we made an impact.

Good serving projects factor this value into everything.
Sometimes even the people you're serving will recognize
it and make sure there are plenty of tangible things for
your group to do. They're the kind of projects you want to
take a group photo in front of.

Is it necessary, though?

During a mission trip my son and I went on together,
one of our hosts sifted through the suitcases of supplies
we brought. We were fine just passing it all along, but he
assumed we'd want a picture with the kids who would
receive a specific pair of shoes we'd donated. It was
admittedly awkward when he had us pose for a photo
while passing along the shoes to the boy, as if we were all
frozen in time.

It's easy to assume that everyone wants to tell a story.

Biblical serving, on the other hand, raises an important question: "If I get nothing out of this or can't tell a before-and-after story, will I serve anyway?"

You know the right answer is "Yes." Your students may even know that. Still, have you developed a perspective for how it will feel if there is no pat on the back or noticeable difference after all the time you served?

Consider that Jesus uttered the phrase "It is finished" while on the cross,[5] yet all of these facts remained:

- Not every person in the world had become a Christ-follower yet—and still he said this.

- Not every individual standing in front of him believed he was the Messiah—and still he said this.

- Not every "project" had been accomplished— and still he said this.

What's the takeaway?

Serve faithfully "before," even if you don't personally get to see the fruit "after." You may even want to end every project saying, "It is finished" to amplify these values:

- **WASTED TIME IS NEVER WASTED TIME:**
Jesus lived among us for 30 years before he
began his teaching ministry. Have you ever felt
it odd that he spent three decades working a
trade? Couldn't he have just given up his life on
the first day he came to earth as a baby and still
have been the perfect sacrifice for our sins?

You know the answer. It's what you tell
teenagers when they explain how they're
tempted and you remind them that Jesus was
also tempted. Instead of giving into those urges,
he lived without sin.[6] Sometimes you seemingly
"waste" time because it has a larger purpose
that keeps it from being wasted.

That means in serving you just *may* need to
fill holes and dig new ones for reasons that
don't make sense to you. Instead of building
something that can be seen, you're building
credibility that can be felt. This may take a
long, long time in situations where suspicion is
more common than trust. In fact, you and your
students might only "till the soil" so a second
group can come in and get all the credit.

Are you OK with that?

- **IT'S OK TO BE ONE LINE IN THE STORY:** Serving isn't about getting others to fix their eyes on your efforts or team but on Christ. What you're doing may just be a punctuation mark in a much greater essay God is authoring. You will experience tremendous freedom if you embrace it, because the weight of everything isn't on your shoulders. If you don't get to finish a project, it's likely that someone else can and will.

  That's not an excuse to not give your best, just the realization that you make a difference by doing something today that someone else is meant to finish tomorrow. Be aware of that so you serve well without pushing too hard to do everything and creating a grumpy group of teenagers who do more harm than good in representing Jesus.

- **PRACTICE "GOD SIGHTINGS":** Take note of how God is present in every act of serving by talking about it together. You can do this through large-group debriefs or by assigning each person a secret prayer partner to pray for and to write notes of encouragement for, talking about how Jesus is being revealed as they serve. There are God Sightings just waiting to be noticed, even if it's simply in the fact that someone decided to honor Jesus by serving.

The upside is that everything and everyone has the fingerprints of the Creator on them. When we focus on caring about the things Jesus cares most about, we make it easier for others to see him through us. Serving shows how the kingdom of God isn't a religious idea but that it's focused on caring for the poor, feeding the hungry, refreshing the thirsty, pursuing the abandoned, rescuing the enslaved, and proclaiming restoration in everything.

Psalm 84:10 proclaims, "A single day in your courts is better than a thousand anywhere else! I would rather be a gatekeeper in the house of my God than live the good life in the homes of the wicked."

Read that again.

And then read it again.

What if you and your teenagers began to look at serving this way?

For real.

❯ A VETERAN LEADER'S PERSPECTIVE *Doug Franklin*

Here's another before-and-after angle to consider...

BEFORE YOU SERVE: Service opportunities allow teenagers to embody what Scripture says about how we should live our lives. However, going on a mission trip is not enough. One week of service in another country is a good start, but we should be more concerned with the other 51 weeks of the year. Students must develop a lifestyle of service. This is why I think pre-trip training and post-trip debriefing are the most important parts of a service trip; they extend the service mindset and kingdom focus into the daily grind of students' lives.

Most pre-trip training is about logistics—a huge mistake. Youth workers focus on logistics because those frighten us the most. We fear that we forgot about a payment, a parent permission form, or a receipt. These mistakes, without question, can doom the trip. We also focus on logistics because we understand them; they are concrete and non-negotiable. We feel more comfortable talking about the calendar than about what Scripture says about service.

If we really want the service experience to transform teenagers, logistics are not going to make it happen. Let's dig into why Jesus served. Let's train ourselves to build strong relationships so our message will be received well. Let's remind students that the only answer we have for others is the truth that Jesus loves them.

AFTER YOU SERVE: At the end of a mission trip, your students will either fall off the mountaintop experience or slowly rappel down. Almost all mission trips give students a spiritual high. The question is, how will they get off the mountain once they're back home?

If you debrief the experience well, you give teenagers the chance to intentionally rappel down the mountain to a new place of spiritual growth. If you don't, they will come crashing down and land in the same spiritual valley they were in before the trip.

Don't give in to the temptation to make your debrief a summary of what happened. Food, weather, and "that one time we saw that guy do that wacky thing" are all short-lived memories. Focus instead on milestones, which are made by applying what we learned to the future. Ask questions like, "What did you learn?" and "How are you going to live differently?" Students should get alone with a pen and paper and ask God to reveal truths they can read over and over as journal entries. A good debrief gives teenagers space and time to hear God after the emotion of the trip has cleared.

THE SKINNY

ON

SERVICE

CHAPTER ③

Putting

It Into

Practice

THE SKINNY

 ON

SERVICE

At some point you'll realize you have blind spots when it comes to serving.

Perhaps you're a creature of habit, nurturing repetition without realizing it. Maybe you plan experiences that extroverts thrive in but squelch introverts at every turn. It's possible you regularly wrestle with the temptation to make your mark and reinvent the wheel.

On the other hand, your blind spots may be more personalized. You may unintentionally remove dignity from the people you're serving by making it seem like you're doing them a grand favor somehow. Those very people may even comply by posing with you in pictures that they'd rather not be in but feel they have no voice to express that to you.

Who or what will help you process through all of that?

Serving is meant to develop Christ-following people—so be that kind of person.

Some would say it begins by letting go and trusting others. It's a fair thought, especially since you'll bump into more needs than you can meet. You'll like the idea of having an entourage around you or when your efforts show up in the local newspaper. It'll appear as if you have momentum and accountability (even if all you have are others around you who won't really challenge your personality or intentions).

Others might say true growth and stretching happen by doing things or using tools you've never competently done or used before. You'll be dared to venture into neighborhoods and cultures that you've never experienced or that make you feel uneasy. You will encounter real spiritual warfare that you will need real spiritual maturity to address.

Whatever the case may be, at some point you'll likely be in over your head because of what you're actually able to do and how it might not completely align with what you had planned to do. That's when it helps to have an accurate view of what serving means individually and collectively.

GENERAL SERVING OPPORTUNITIES

Some serving opportunities will be more about meeting tangible, physical needs, while other opportunities will more directly address unseen spiritual or emotional needs. All of your efforts can matter, but Jesus' strategy still should serve as an anchor. Consider your "Jerusalem, Judea, Samaria, and ends of the earth" as you process through the different general ways to serve:

- **PROGRAMS:** Call it a youth group, a student ministry, or whatever is the newest "right" term to summarize the way you serve the teenagers in your area. Some churches develop a midweek program while others rely on Sunday school or small groups. However you do it, offer regular opportunities for students to serve. Make the most of this ongoing opportunity by developing serving opportunities at all levels, be it standing on a stage or preparing attendance papers.

In one youth group I led, our student and adult servant-leaders gathered the night before every program to read the Bible together, pray for area teenagers, and prep to serve. It all fostered an amazing community that was open to every student who served. In turn, we fostered a community-within-the-community—people who were aware of how God significantly works through seemingly insignificant details.

Potential downside: Teenagers who serve in your weekly program may feel or appear more important than other students who simply attend. Their bond can also appear like a clique, and the influence they have on their best days and worst days can have an exclusive impact that you may not be able to control. Nurture their character, and assign mentors to every core area of the ministry.

- **PROJECTS:** We find plenty of examples in the Bible of people who come in, do something for God, and leave the pages of Scripture. Projects are just that: one-shot serving events or undertakings where you do what needs to be done in a short amount of time. You can create your own projects without outside help, but the best experiences allow for experienced partners to handle core details and logistics on your behalf.

Potential downside: Projects sometimes become "good deeds" that you show up for and do, and then you go home afterward. It will be up to you to explain to your team and those you're serving, "We're doing this because God loves you and cares about what's happening here." There's also the possibility your project will create problems with property owners where you're serving or with other local churches that have pre-existing partnerships there. Take a trip beforehand to wherever you plan to serve and scout out the potential for this well in advance of your project.

- **PARTNERSHIPS:** The difference between a project and a partnership is that you see something in a partner's vision or need that makes you want to connect for the long haul. Think of it like moving from casual dating to a committed relationship. Sometimes projects become partnerships, and other times partnerships dissolve into projects. The sign of a good opportunity is when your students' journey with Jesus and each other has prepared them to partner with this ministry so that growth happens in ways that only God can explain—and in ways that only God can get the glory.

Potential downside: Make sure whomever you're serving doesn't become financially or tangibly co-dependent on your efforts. Unless God leads you otherwise, look for opportunities that are supported by a network of groups, or else you may end up feeling pressured to do more than you can. That can also make it difficult to dissolve your partnership if you feel God leading you to do other things as a ministry down the road.

- **ADVOCACY:** It's no secret that teenagers like to personalize their life, from the phone they use to the clothes they wear. Advocacy is one way to let them become champions for whatever cause they want to adopt, whether it's using a water jug to raise money for kids in Africa who need water or running a race where sponsors donate money per mile. This is like the hybrid between a project and a partnership because you can serve several needs at the same time—or at any time. People taking an advocacy approach may decide to continue until they see a certain kind of result or simply until they feel led to do something else.

Potential downside: Sending money isn't meant to replace the command to "go" that Jesus shared in the Great Commission.[7] Our calling isn't just to support ideas but to step out in faith and share the good news of Jesus so that more people can become his disciples. If you're not carefully, advocacy can skip this clear command by Christ himself.

Always be aware of how your serving efforts might overlap with someone else's serving efforts. You'll save yourself much time and heartache by humbly learning from others who are already "on the ground." Their strengths can complement your weaknesses, whether you do better with the big picture or the details. No matter how you look at it, someone knows *something* better than you do. Use this to your advantage as you choose between the various connections you can form.

This may mean sitting down with your church leadership for ideas on where to start. Whether you're looking overseas or another part of this country, your church or denomination may already support a network of missionaries who could benefit from your service. Neighboring churches or social media can also be helpful in identifying some of the more pressing needs. As a backup plan, seek out people who are in need and ask them where they normally turn for help. That alone may give you a lead on which groups to approach for future projects, partnerships, and advocacy.

Remain teachable in this process, asking questions and taking notes. Once you feel you're able to jump in somewhere, propose the opportunity to your ministry leaders and students, and tackle it together. (You may want to engage parents and church leaders in the conversation, too.) Let them affirm that this opportunity aligns with your youth ministry's mission, calling, and personality. It all tracks back to making sure the internal side of serving comes before the external. Join God in what he's already doing—don't be consumed by trying to prove you can do things better than everyone else.

OVERLOOKED SERVING OPPORTUNITIES

When we serve other people, we are serving God.

When we ignore opportunities to serve other people, we are ignoring opportunities to serve God.

Serving is often about seeing and responding to the daily needs around us. It's easy to overlook these opportunities when we have a certain way we expect things to be, look, or play out. But Jesus looked at people that the world overlooked and served them with his full attention. He even challenged the most religious people in his culture to hang out with him—and with the overlooked.

This raises an important question: Who or what are your serving efforts likely to overlook?

- **ENGAGE THE ORDINARY:** It's exciting to be a part of a service project that's unique or different. We all have enough chores at home that don't seem glamorous, which perhaps is why it can be hard to do things for Jesus the closer you get to home. As Jesus reminded his disciples, the problem is not that there isn't a harvest right in front of us, but that "the workers are few."[8] Sometimes we don't step forward into things we're already a part of because we're tired of them, too familiar with them, or unsure how we can really make a difference.

Life is not found in sidestepping our daily challenges and opportunities but in journeying deeper into them. Teenagers don't need to give a grand speech about it; they simply need to serve their friends, family, coaches, or bosses as Jesus would. It might involve a special act of kindness, but more likely it means saying or doing something they've procrastinated saying or doing.

GUT CHECK: How willing are you to help teenagers see that they may need to take a pass on the next serving opportunity you're organizing so they can instead invest time in their household, neighborhood, friendships,

workplace, extracurricular activities, or school?

- **SERVE THE SEEMINGLY NON-BROKEN:**
  In the story of the prodigal son in Luke 15, we see how his wild living has left him broken. On the other hand, the older brother in the parable doesn't seem quite as "broken" as his sibling. He certainly comes across as moody and jealous when the father throws a huge "welcome home" party for the younger rebel. The older brother also needs restoration, but we are easily tempted to skip over that without a second look.

  Some serving experiences play out like this because we focus all of our efforts on the more dramatic needs, skipping "older brother" opportunities along the way. The person who volunteered to be your site leader or point person on the other side has needs you can meet. Perhaps even some of the student or adult leaders in your midst are grumbling because they have gaps in their own lives and the idea of serving someone else is making them bitter. These are opportunities to minister and serve.

  GUT CHECK: How many opportunities in front of you don't appear like opportunities because someone or something seems to

be doing fine? What does it mean to take a second look at these people or projects?

- **CONNECT THE DOTS:** Serving, in itself, may not lead someone to Jesus. But what is certain is that a lack of serving will lead no one to Jesus. An explanation can help people connect the dots, whether you cultivate a long dialogue with those you impact or simply say, "I'm doing this because I love you, and because God loves you."

  Likewise, teenagers who are following Jesus will need to learn or remember the theological realities of why they serve. Some people do things to try to "repay God" for what he's done for us. We could never, ever repay Jesus for dying on the cross for us, which is one reason why his grace is so amazing. Try to help students see serving less as a way to impress God or relieve guilt and more of an opportunity to practically stay centered on Jesus.

  GUT CHECK: In what ways has serving begun appearing as something it isn't because of conversations that aren't happening?

- **FURTHER INTERGENERATIONAL CONNECTIONS:** Teenagers who serve tend to become open to the adults on the trip, whether they see these adults as temporary leaders for the day or as future friends they can continue to connect with. Seize this opportunity and match them together so that the leaders will want to keep coming around and the teenagers become open to the adults' potential for mentoring and influence.

A similar idea is likewise true, as teenagers who have a great serving experience with their church are more likely to remain plugged in beyond the youth ministry. The success they felt jumping into their project can give them the confidence they need to jump into an ongoing volunteer role or task. When more students want to serve, the church is inspired; when the church is inspired, more students will want to serve.

GUT CHECK: What impact is your youth ministry having on the adults of your church? What impact are the adults of your church having on your youth ministry?

- **SERVE YOUR STUDENTS' FAMILIES:** Serving opportunities usually require parents entrusting you with their kids, whether they're being dropped off to serve in your band or your team is traveling to another country. Don't take advantage of this trust or let it go unappreciated. Take the time to address the small stuff and the big picture, whether or not the parent thinks to ask for it.

Remember that you're trying to come alongside parents, not demanding they come alongside you. Many of them want to see their child's life changed, just as you do. Others simply want their son or daughter to have as many positive experiences as possible during adolescence. Don't be afraid to invite parents into your serving efforts, provided it wouldn't become counterproductive to the students.

GUT CHECK: Do you tend to view dealing with parents as a serving opportunity or as a necessary evil? Why?

- **HONOR YOUR ADULT LEADERS:** All trips need chaperones, but your truer, deeper need is a group of quality, Jesus-centered adult leaders who make investments beyond maintaining the rules. Show them the proper respect by engaging them in your plans. I blew this on one mission trip when we drove through the town I grew up in and kept randomly stopping our caravan to get donuts, slushies, and more. I intended it to be a spontaneous lesson on how when God doesn't explain what he's doing, we'll either choose to see what irritates us or how he's blessing us. But I didn't let my adults know this ahead of time, so they reacted with frustration instead of support—a natural reaction under the circumstances.

One thing I believe we have done right over the years is to make sure our adult leaders don't have to pay out of their own pocket for mission trips. Do whatever math you can on this, such as spreading those costs among the overall price tag teenagers must pay. Make sure you publicly thank these leaders, their spouses, and their other family members for allowing them to serve with you.

GUT CHECK: How can you tell when your adult leaders really feel like serving is bringing them life?

➲ A VETERAN LEADER'S PERSPECTIVE *Doug Franklin*

When adults go on service experiences with students, they often struggle to find their role. Are they taskmasters, cheerleaders, or quality control? Giving them a defined role can make their experience great. Challenge adults to use service opportunities to build relationships with teenagers. They want to jump in and work, but by getting to know students they will see longer-term benefits. Most of the year, we struggle to find meaningful time with students, and these experiences provide uninterrupted time away from distractions.

Train your adult leaders to ask students "discovery" questions. Teenagers have a favorite subject: themselves. Encourage adult leaders to ask students about their lives, their interests, and how they describe their faith. Students connect to people who care about them and sacrifice their time. Once teenagers know you care, they will listen to what you say and will let you speak hard truth in their lives. Mission trips and service experiences are the perfect opportunities to form those deep relationships.

FORMING STUDENT AND ADULT SERVING TEAMS

It's risky to entrust ministry to other people.

They won't see or do things like you would. They will have a different definition of success. They may say something in one moment that offsets lengthy investments you've made.

Do it anyway.

The Bible says we're called to train our youth to follow the right path, and we also need to entrust what we've learned into other adults.[9] Both of those efforts require a mutual commitment to whatever you sense is required. Be clear on what you expect, considering several specific values up front:

- **Honor God:** Don't confuse your cause for Christ. The former is what you do; the latter is who you do it for.

- **Set the pace:** Challenge yourself to serve before you challenge anyone else. It's much easier to lead someone somewhere you're already going.

- **Merge the secular and sacred:** Serving with a church or youth group isn't a "more important task" than the other parts of our lives. Help teenagers discover how every area of life is sacred, whether they're taking part in a mission trip, helping a random kid do his homework, or honoring a day off with their family.

- **Draw a dramatic line:** If someone says they're interested in serving in the youth ministry, smile and hand them a pair of gloves. Explain that you (or another leader) will go with them to a local high school to pick up trash until both bags are full—and while there, you'll talk about what it really means to serve teenagers.

- **Create a covenant:** Find people of character who will help you discern what is realistic to ask of anyone who serves. Write it down, keep it simple, and include specific details about the commitment and character that is expected. Require every person who serves (including you) to fill it out and sign it.

- **Train from every angle:** Have a weekly, bi-weekly, or monthly training time everyone is required to attend. Ask everyone to bring a thought, quote, or short article to share with the group. Tackle a wide range of topics: theology, spiritual disciples, responses to crisis situations, what's happening in youth culture, and so on.

- **Pray with each other:** It's one thing to pray *for* each other, and another thing to pray *with* each other. Circle up, grab hands, and have each person say the name of another person they feel called to serve.

Remember that serving is a privilege. Some people who say they want to serve really just want to feel valued. Help them to sort out the difference. After all, God says we're valuable not because of what we do but because of who he is. God is self-sufficient and doesn't need us to serve, but we get to serve because it's one way the world can get to know him.

TWO FINAL THOUGHTS YOU MAY NOT WANT TO HEAR

Anything you do for Jesus isn't as important as Jesus himself.

That's the first thing you need to take in and process:

> *"Yes, everything else is worthless when compared with the infinite value of knowing Christ Jesus my Lord. For his sake I have discarded everything else, counting it all as garbage, so that I could gain Christ"* (Philippians 3:8).

The Apostle Paul did great, amazing things for God. He had been a prominent Jew and Pharisee. As a Christian, he passionately strengthened and furthered the church. Still, he pointed out that there was something more important than all of that serving.

Jesus. It has to be Jesus. If you forget him, you neglect him.

That doesn't seem hard to remember, yet if we aren't careful, we can lose sight of him in all of the serving projects we help coordinate.

And that leads to the second thing you may not want to hear.

Your hands should be wet and dirty.

Your hands.

John 13 reveals that on the night that Christ was betrayed and arrested, he showed his disciples the full extent of his love. This guest of honor stood up during the Last Supper, stripped down to his most basic garments, and began scrubbing the feet of his followers.

All of them, including Judas.

This is how greatness is defined.

Jesus explained:

> *"And since I, your Lord and Teacher, have washed your feet, you ought to wash each other's feet. I have given you an example to follow. Do as I have done to you" (John 13:14-15).*

If you don't serve in the trenches but simply lead from above, youth ministry will become your reason to not do what you're asking students to do.

You can easily spend all your time trying to get teenagers to take a bold step with God that you don't actually take yourself. You'll say, "Share Jesus with your friends! Bring them with you to church!" How often are you regularly doing those things with your own peers or neighbors?

Maybe you feel you're so busy serving students that you don't have time to sit in "big church." Perhaps you feel so deeply called to your niche that you don't know where to start with other adults.

Teenagers don't need another pep talk from you on how to serve their generation. They need to watch you be an example in serving your generation.

You know this won't be easy, and you may have excuses lined up. Then again, maybe you don't. Maybe your limitations will drive you to give it that much more effort.

My wife and I are not gifted at this. We were at a block party in our neighborhood and found it harder to talk with the other adults than with the teenagers on our street. That didn't stop us from trying, though. We've even printed out a map of our neighborhood so we could write the names of our neighbors over each house and pray for them by name. We've created and looked for opportunities to serve them, from mowing someone's grass to installing a basketball hoop so the neighborhood kids could play anytime.

The ideas are limitless, but the values are simple:

- **Be visible:** Instead of reading a book on the couch, head to the porch and read it outside. Be sure to say "Hi!" to those who walk by.

- **Make some noise:** Crank up some familiar music when you're working on a project outside. Music can help people feel you're approachable.

- **Buddy up:** Share chores with your neighbors, such as helping them with a big project or asking them to help you with yours. Spring for lunch either way.

- **Take them up on it:** If a neighbor has said, "If you need anything, just ask," go ahead and ask. Sometimes you build a friendship by helping someone else feel needed.

- **Make no excuses:** If you live in an apartment or in an area where homes are far apart, organize a board game night in your home or a community room where you provide ice cream sandwiches and the games.

I say this with full confidence: Serving others like this will be more fruitful than you can imagine. Fold it into your family's DNA and have conversations about it. Be known as the house that always has ice cream bars on hand and a campfire in the driveway.

Teenagers aren't just looking for a great youth worker— they're looking for a Christ-follower who is leaving footsteps they can step into.

They won't know how to wash feet unless they see you doing it first.

I think you get the picture.

BE the church.

ENDNOTES

[1] See Matthew 20:32, Mark 10:36, 51, and Luke 18:41.

[2] apostle1.com/oofm-rule-of-life.htm

[3] Edward K. Rowell (editor), *1001 Quotes, Illustrations, and Humorous Stories for Preachers, Teachers, and Writers* (Grand Rapids, MI: Baker Books, 2008), 60.

[4] See Mark 5:21-43.

[5] See John 19:30.

[6] See Hebrews 4:15.

[7] See Matthew 28:16-20.

[8] See Luke 10:2.

[9] See Proverbs 22:6 and 2 Timothy 2:2.